Learning about Cats

THE
OCICAT

by Joanne Mattern

Consultant:
Kate Bynum
President
Ocicats of North America

CAPSTONE
HIGH-INTEREST
BOOKS

an imprint of Capstone Press
Mankato, Minnesota

Capstone High-Interest Books are published by Capstone Press
151 Good Counsel Drive, P.O. Box 669, Mankato, Minnesota 56002
http://www.capstone-press.com

Library of Congress Cataloging-in-Publication Data
Mattern, Joanne, 1963–
    The Ocicat/by Joanne Mattern.
    p. cm.—(Learning about cats)
    Summary: Discusses the history, development, habits, and care of the Ocicat, a
domestic cat breed known for its wild appearance and pleasant personality.
    Includes bibliographical references (p. 45) and index.
    ISBN 0-7368-1302-0 (hardcover)
    1. Ocicat—Juvenile literature. [1. Ocicat. 2. Cats. 3. Pets.] I. Title. II. Series.
SF449.O35 M38 2003
636.8'2—dc21   2001008339

Editorial Credits

Gillia Olson, editor; Linda Clavel, series designer and illustrator; Gene Bentdahl,
    book designer; Jo Miller, photo researcher

Photo Credits

Chanan Photography, cover, 4, 6, 14, 23, 24, 30, 35, 38, 40–41
Larry Johnson, 10, 29
Photo by Mark McCullough, 16
U.S. Fish and Wildlife Service/Tom Smylie, 12
www.ronkimballstock.com, 8, 19, 20, 26, 32, 37

1 2 3 4 5 6 07 06 05 04 03 02

Table of Contents

Quick Facts about the Ocicat

Description

Size: Ocicats are medium-sized cats.

Weight: A full-grown Ocicat weighs between 6 and 14 pounds (2.7 and 6.4 kilograms).

Physical features: The Ocicat has a short, glossy coat. Its wedge-shaped head has a short nose and a wide face. An Ocicat's body is muscular, long, and sleek.

Color: Ocicats have dark spots on a lighter background color. Background colors include tawny, honey, brown, cream, and silver.

Development

Place of origin: The Ocicat breed began in the United States.

History of breed: The first Ocicat was born in 1964. It was part Siamese and part Abyssinian.

Numbers: In 2001, 646 Ocicats were registered in North America with the Cat Fanciers' Association (CFA). Owners who register their Ocicats list the cats' breeding records with an official club. The CFA is the world's largest organization of cat breeders.

Chapter 1

The Ocicat

The Ocicat's spotted coat makes it look like a wildcat. But the Ocicat does not have a wild personality. It is friendly and affectionate. The Ocicat is healthy and needs little special care.

Appearance

The Ocicat's body is strong and sleek. Males usually weigh from 11 to 14 pounds (5 to 6.4 kilograms). Females are smaller. They usually weigh between 6 and 10 pounds (2.7 and 4.5 kilograms).

The Ocicat has a wedge-shaped head. Its ears are broad and may have pointed tufts of hair at the tips. Its almond-shaped eyes angle toward the ears.

Ocicats may look like wildcats, but they are friendly and affectionate.

The Ocicat's fur is short and glossy. Its coat is ticked. Each hair has bands of color. The Ocicat's coat has a dark spotted pattern on a lighter background color.

An Ocicat can have one of a variety of color patterns. These colors include chocolate, cinnamon, and blue. Cinnamon is a red-brown color. Blue is a shade of gray.

Personality

Ocicats are friendly and curious. They seem to like to be around people. They usually are very interested in their surroundings. Ocicats get along well with children and will play games with them.

Ocicats are social animals. They seem to prefer to be around other cats. Ocicats also get along well with dogs.

Ocicats often follow their owners from room to room. Some Ocicats will ride on their owners' shoulders.

Ocicats are smart. They sometimes can be trained to do tricks and walk on a leash.

Ocicats' strong legs help them explore their surroundings.

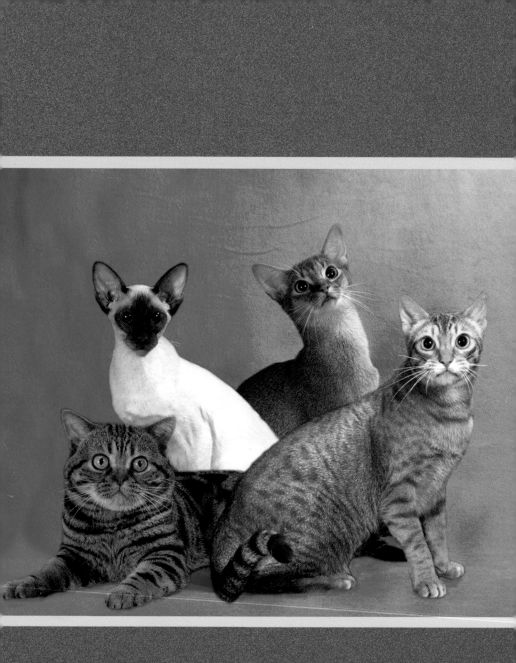

Chapter 2

Development of the Breed

The Ocicat is a fairly new breed. It began about 40 years ago. Ocicats are mostly Siamese. But they also are part Abyssinian.

Tonga

In 1964, a Michigan cat breeder named Virginia Daly was trying to produce a Siamese cat with Abyssinian points. Points are dark areas of fur on a cat's ears, face, tail, and feet. Abyssinians have ticked coats. Each hair has bands of light and dark color. People also call this type of coat "agouti."

Daly first bred an Abyssinian and a Siamese cat. She then bred one of the kittens to a Siamese. She bred one of these kittens to another Siamese. One of the kittens from this

The American Shorthair (bottom left), chocolate point Siamese (top left), and Abyssinian (top right) have been bred to create today's Ocicat (bottom right).

Virginia Daly's daughter named the first Ocicat after the ocelot (above).

mating had white fur and golden spots. Daly named the cat Tonga. Daly's daughter called him an "ocicat" because Tonga looked like a wildcat called the ocelot. Daly sold Tonga as a pet. Tonga was neutered so he could not reproduce.

Daly then wrote to Dr. Clyde Keeler of Georgia University. Dr. Keeler was interested in creating a cat that looked like the Egyptian

Spotted Fishing Cat. This extinct cat lived in ancient Egypt.

Daly told Dr. Keeler that she had produced a spotted cat through one of her breedings. Daly bred Tonga's parents again. They produced more spotted kittens.

A New Breed

Other breeders began working with Ocicats. They bred some Ocicats with American Shorthairs. Genes from American Shorthairs passed the traits of a large, strong body to the Ocicat.

Ocicats began appearing at cat shows in the late 1960s. The International Cat Association (TICA) officially recognized the breed in 1986. In 1987, the Cat Fanciers' Association (CFA) recognized the Ocicat. Since then, the Ocicat has become very popular at cat shows. Many Ocicats have won championships.

Chapter 3

Today's Ocicat

Today, the Ocicat is becoming more popular in the United States and Canada. Many people like the cat's wild appearance and pleasant personality.

Breed Standard

Judges look for specific physical features when they judge an Ocicat at a cat show. These features are called the breed standard.

In general, an ideal Ocicat is strong and powerful. Its body is solid and muscular. An Ocicat's dense bones and muscles make it feel heavier than it looks. The cat's legs are long and muscular. The shoulders and chest are deep and broad. Its tail is long and slim with a dark tip.

Ocicats should be muscular, with a broad chest and powerful legs.

The Cat Fanciers' Asso

Judge: B BRADSHA

2

Ring #

The World's Largest Registry of Pedigree

The Ocicat's head is wedge-shaped. An Ocicat has almond-shaped eyes. Its large ears may have small tufts of hair at the tips.

An ideal Ocicat's coat is short, smooth, glossy, and covered with spots. An Ocicat can score more points in cat shows if its spots are very well-defined. They also have an M-shaped marking on their forehead and dark markings around their eyes.

Some Ocicats do not meet the breed standard. These cats may be solid colored or have tabby stripes rather than spots. Ocicats without spots cannot compete in cat shows. Ocicats with blue eyes are also disqualified from cat shows. But these cats make excellent pets.

Colors

The CFA accepts Ocicats in 12 color patterns. The spots always are darker than the rest of the fur. All Ocicats have agouti coats. Background coat colors come in tawny, ivory, honey, blue,

Judges at cat shows rate cats according to how well they meet the breed standard.

and silver. Tawny is a ticked brown color. Silver is almost white.

An Ocicat's spots can be black, chocolate, cinnamon, fawn, blue, or lavender. Fawn is a light shade of the red-brown cinnamon color. Lavender is a lighter shade of chocolate that has a pink tint.

The 12 accepted Ocicat color patterns come from combinations of background and spot colors. Six of the colors are based off the silver background. They are ebony silver, chocolate silver, cinnamon silver, blue silver, lavender silver, and fawn silver. The other six colors have varying backgrounds according to the spot color. These six are tawny, chocolate, cinnamon, blue, lavender, and fawn.

Ocicats come in many colors, including blue (left), chocolate (right), and chocolate silver (bottom).

Chapter 4

Owning an Ocicat

People can find Ocicats in several ways. Most people buy Ocicats from breeders. Breeders often charge several hundred dollars for an Ocicat. Rarely, people adopt Ocicats from animal shelters. Others may adopt from a rescue organization. These cats usually are less expensive than those sold by breeders.

Ocicat Breeders

The best way to find a purebred Ocicat is to go to a breeder. Cat shows are good places to meet breeders. Most breeders are happy to talk to people about their cats.

People also can find breeders in magazines and on the Internet. Cat magazines list breeders' names and phone numbers in ads.

The best way to find purebred Ocicats such as these is to go to a breeder.

Breeders may have their own web sites. Pet stores also may be able to refer people to Ocicat breeders.

People usually buy kittens from breeders. Most breeders own one or both of the kitten's parents. Buyers who see the kitten's parents can learn how the kitten might look and behave when it is fully grown.

Before buying, people should talk to other people who have bought cats from a certain breeder. These references can help people decide if a breeder is responsible. They also should get the medical history of the breeder's cats. These steps will help people purchase healthy cats with good qualities.

Animal Shelters

Some people may want to adopt a cat from an animal shelter. Animal shelters keep unwanted animals and try to find homes for them.

Many people adopt from shelters so they can save animals' lives. Many more animals are brought to shelters than there are people

Seeing a kitten's mother may help a buyer learn how the kitten will look and behave when it is grown.

available to adopt them. Animals that are not adopted often are euthanized. Shelter workers euthanize animals by injecting them with substances that stop their breathing or heartbeat.

Animal shelters often charge less for cats than breeders do. Most shelters charge only a small fee for animal adoptions. Local veterinarians often provide discounts on medical services for shelter animals.

Shelters rarely have purebred Ocicats such as this lavender Ocicat.

Shelters almost always have mixed-breed cats available for adoption. Cats from shelters rarely are registered. Purebred Ocicats are registered.

Many good pets are available at animal shelters. People who do not plan to breed or show their cat can find a good pet at a shelter.

Rescue Organizations

People who would like to save an unwanted cat but want to adopt a purebred Ocicat can contact a rescue organization. Rescue organizations find homes for unwanted or neglected animals.

Rescue organizations usually specialize in just one or two breeds. They rarely euthanize the animals. Instead, they care for the animals until they are adopted.

Rescue organizations offer a good alternative for people who do not plan to show their Ocicat. People usually pay less for an Ocicat from a rescue organization than for one from a breeder. People may even find registered cats when adopting from a rescue organization.

People can find information about rescue organizations in several ways. They often have Internet sites. They also may advertise in magazines or newspapers. Animal shelters and pet stores also may refer people to rescue organizations.

Chapter 5

Caring for an Ocicat

Ocicats are a strong, healthy breed. With good care, Ocicats can live 15 to 20 years.

Indoor and Outdoor Cats

Cats usually live longer, healthier lives if they are kept inside. Some cat owners let their cats roam outdoors. Cats that roam outdoors often catch serious diseases from other cats. Outdoor cats may be injured by cars or other animals.

Both indoor and outdoor cats mark their territories by scratching objects to leave their scent. Cats also scratch to release tension and to sharpen their claws. When cats scratch indoors, they can damage furniture, carpets, or curtains. To prevent damage, owners should provide their cats with a scratching post. They

Owners can provide items such as cat houses to help their Ocicats live comfortably.

can buy a scratching post at a pet store or make one from wood and carpet.

People who keep their cats inside must also provide a litter box where the cat can eliminate bodily wastes. Owners should clean the waste out of the box each day and change the litter at least once each week. Cats may refuse to use a dirty litter box.

Feeding

Like all cats, Ocicats need a high-quality cat food. Owners can choose to feed their cat dry or moist cat food. The amount of food needed depends on the individual cat's size and appetite.

Dry food usually is less expensive than moist food. Dry food can help keep cats' teeth clean. It will not spoil if it is left in a dish.

Owners who feed their cats moist food usually feed them twice each day. This type of food can spoil easily. It should not be left out for more than one hour.

A high-quality, dry cat food can help keep an Ocicat's teeth clean.

Both dry and moist food are suitable for Ocicats. Cats may prefer one type of food. Owners can ask their veterinarian or breeder which type of food is best for their cats.

Cats need to drink plenty of water to stay healthy. Owners should make sure their cats' water bowls are always filled. The water should be changed each day to keep it fresh and clean.

Grooming

An Ocicat's short coat needs little grooming. This cat should be brushed once each week. Owners should use a soft bristle brush to remove loose hair.

After brushing, owners should use a coarse comb to smooth out the cat's fur. Some owners rub their Ocicats with a soft cloth called a chamois to keep their fur shiny.

Regular brushing helps prevent hairballs. When a cat cleans itself, it swallows loose pieces of fur. Fur can form balls in the cat's stomach. The cat must vomit the ball. Sometimes, large hairballs block the cat's digestive system. These hairballs require surgery to be removed. Brushing removes loose fur before the cat can swallow it.

Jellied medicines also can prevent hairballs. The jelly coats hairballs in the cat's stomach and helps them pass harmlessly in the cat's waste.

All Ocicats, such as this fawn silver Ocicat, usually need little grooming.

Good care can help Ocicats remain healthy throughout their lives.

Nail Care

The tip of a cat's claw is called the nail. Like other cats, Ocicats need to have their nails trimmed every few weeks. This practice reduces damage if cats claw the carpet or furniture.

A cat can get ingrown nails if its nails are not trimmed regularly. Ingrown nails can occur when a cat does not sharpen its claws often.

The claws can grow into the pad or bottom of the paw. This growth can cause serious and painful infections.

Owners should begin trimming a cat's nails when it is a kitten. The kitten will become used to having its nails trimmed as it grows older. Veterinarians can show owners how to trim their cats' nails with a special nail clipper.

Dental Care

All cats need regular dental care to protect their teeth and gums from plaque. This coating of bacteria and saliva causes tooth decay and gum disease.

Owners also should brush their cat's teeth at least once a week. They can use a cloth or a special toothbrush made for cats. Owners should never brush their cat's teeth with toothpaste made for people. It can make the cat sick. Instead, they can buy special toothpaste for cats at pet stores.

As cats grow older, they may have more plaque and other dental problems. Owners should then have a veterinarian clean a cat's teeth. Veterinarians have special tools and supplies to clean animals' teeth.

Veterinarian Visits
Ocicats should have regular checkups by a veterinarian. Most veterinarians recommend yearly visits for cats. Older cats may need to visit the veterinarian two or three times each year. Older cats are more likely to develop health problems than younger cats. More frequent checkups help the veterinarian find and treat these problems.

People who adopt an adult Ocicat may want to take it to a veterinarian as soon as possible for a checkup. The veterinarian will check the cat's heart, lungs, internal organs, eyes, ears, mouth, and coat. A checkup is important for cats whose medical history is unknown. Other cats may not have had a checkup recently.

Owners also may need to get vaccinations for their Ocicat or kitten. Breeders usually make sure kittens have their first round of vaccinations. Vaccinations are shots of

Regular veterinary checkups can help keep Ocicats healthy.

medicine that help prevent serious diseases. These vaccinations prevent diseases such as rabies, feline panleukopenia, and feline leukemia.

Rabies is a deadly disease that is spread by animal bites. Both people and animals can die from rabies. Most states and provinces have laws that require owners to vaccinate their cats against rabies.

Feline panleukopenia also is called feline distemper. This virus causes fever, vomiting, and death.

Feline leukemia attacks a cat's immune system. The cat is unable to fight off infections and other illnesses. Feline leukemia is spread through a cat's bodily fluids. Owners who show their cats often vaccinate them against feline leukemia.

Spaying and Neutering

Veterinarians also spay and neuter cats. These surgeries remove the cat's reproductive organs so the cats cannot reproduce. Owners who do not plan to breed their cats should have them spayed or neutered. These surgeries keep unwanted kittens from being born.

Spay and neuter surgeries may have other benefits. They may prevent diseases of the reproductive organs. Spayed and neutered cats usually have calmer personalities than cats that are not spayed or neutered. They also are less likely to wander away from home.

Healthy Ocicats are alert. They have bright eyes and shiny coats.

The Tame "Wildcat"

Ocicats are known for their wild appearance and fun personality. Since the 1960s, Ocicats have grown in popularity. They have won many championships in cat shows.

People who want a healthy cat that is easy to care for can consider adopting an Ocicat. These spotted cats can provide years of companionship.

People who want a cat that is easy to care for may want to adopt an Ocicat.

CHOCOLATE OCICAT

Long,
thin tail

Spotted
coat

Tabby "M" marking

Wedge-shaped head

Quick Facts about Cats

A male cat is called a tom. A female cat is called a queen. A young cat is called a kitten. A family of kittens born at one time is called a litter.

Origin: Shorthaired cat breeds descended from a type of African wildcat called *Felis lybica*. Longhaired breeds may have descended from Asian wildcats. People domesticated or tamed these breeds as early as 1500 B.C.

Types: The Cat Fanciers' Association accepts 40 domestic cat breeds for competition. The smallest breeds weigh about 5 to 7 pounds (2.3 to 3.2 kilograms) when grown. The largest breeds can weigh more than 18 pounds (8.2 kilograms). Cat breeds may be either shorthaired or longhaired. Cats' coats can be a variety of colors. These colors include many shades of white, black, gray, brown, and red.

Reproduction: Most cats are sexually mature at 5 or 6 months. A sexually mature female cat goes into estrus several times each year. Estrus also is called "heat." During this time, she can mate with a male. Kittens are born about 65 days after breeding. An average litter includes four kittens.

Development: Kittens are born blind and deaf. Their eyes open about 10 days after birth. Their hearing develops at the same time. They can live on their own when they are 6 weeks old.

Life span: With good care, cats can live 15 or more years.

Sight: A cat's eyesight is adapted for hunting. Cats are good judges of distance. They see movement more easily than detail. Cats also have excellent night vision.

Hearing: Cats can hear sounds that are too high for humans to hear. A cat can turn its ears to focus on different sounds.

Smell: A cat has an excellent sense of smell. Cats use scents to establish their territories. Cats scratch or rub the sides of their faces against objects. These actions release a scent from glands between their toes or in their skin.

Taste: Cats cannot taste as many foods as people can. For example, cats are not very sensitive to sweet tastes.

Touch: Cats' whiskers are sensitive to touch. Cats use their whiskers to touch objects and sense changes in their surroundings.

Balance: Cats have an excellent sense of balance. They use their tails to help keep their balance. Cats can walk on narrow objects without falling. They usually can right themselves and land on their feet during falls from short distances.

Communication: Cats use many sounds to communicate with people and other animals. They may meow when hungry or hiss when afraid. Cats also purr. Scientists do not know exactly what causes cats to make this sound. Cats often purr when they are relaxed. But they also may purr when they are sick or in pain.

Words to Know

agouti (uh-GOO-tee)—ticked; ticked coats have bands of light and dark color on each hair.

breeder (BREED-ur)—someone who breeds and raises cats or other animals

euthanize (YOO-thuh-nize)—to put an animal to death by injecting it with a substance that stops its breathing or heartbeat

inherit (in-HER-it)—to receive a physical characteristic from parents

neuter (NOO-tur)—to remove a male animal's testicles so it cannot reproduce

spay (SPAY)—to remove a female animal's uterus and ovaries so it cannot reproduce

trait (TRATE)—a quality or characteristic that makes one person or animal different from another

vaccination (vak-suh-NAY-shun)—a shot of medicine that protects a person or animal from disease

To Learn More

Alderton, David. *Cats.* DK Handbooks. New York: DK Publishing, 2000.

McKee, Bill. *The Guide to Owning an Ocicat.* Neptune City, N.J.: T.F.H. Publications, 2001.

Petras, Kathryn, and Ross Petras. *Cats: 47 Favorite Breeds, Appearance, History, Personality, and Lore.* Fandex Family Field Guides. New York: Workman Publishing, 1997.

Rixon, Angela. *The Illustrated Encyclopedia of Cat Breeds.* New York: Smithmark Publishers Inc., 1995.

You can read articles about Ocicats in *Cat Fancy* magazine.

Useful Addresses

American Cat Fanciers Association (ACFA)
P.O. Box 1949
Nixa, MO 65714-1949

Canadian Cat Association (CCA)
289 Rutherford Road South
Unit 18
Brampton, ON L6W 3R9
Canada

Cat Fanciers' Association (CFA)
P.O. Box 1005
Manasquan, NJ 08736-0805

Ocicats of North America
947 South 6th Street
Clinton, IN 47842

Internet Sites

Canadian Cat Association
http://www.cca-afc.com

Care for Pets
http://www.avma.org/care4pets

Cat Fanciers' Association
http://www.cfainc.org

Cats Central
http://www.cats-central.com

Kittycat Corner—Ocicat
http://www.kittycatcorner.com/ocicat.html

Ocicats of North America
http://www.abcs.com/catoninetail/ona

Index